The Great Barrier
REEF
AN UNDERWATER ADVENTURE

SCHOLASTIC INC.

New York   Toronto   London   Auckland   Sydney
Mexico City   New Delhi   Hong Kong   Buenos Aires

• ISBN-13: 978-0-545-01008-5 ISBN-10: 0-545-01008-X • Copyright © 2007 by innovativeKids® • All rights reserved. Published by Scholastic Inc., 557 Broadway, New York, NY 10012, by arrangement with innovativeKids®, a division of innovative USA®, Inc. SCHOLASTIC and associated logos are trademarks and/or registered trademarks of Scholastic Inc. 12 11 10 9 8 7 6 5 4 3 2 1   7 8 9 10 11/0 • Printed in the U.S.A.   23 • First Scholastic printing, January 2007 • Conceived and developed by the creative team at innovativeKids® • Art direction and design by Cheshire Studio

Many thanks to the following experts for their assistance with this book: Rick MacPherson, Program Director, The Coral Reef Alliance; R. Aidan Martin, Director, ReefQuest Centre for Shark Research; Ken Peterson, Senior Public Relations Manager, Monterey Bay Aquarium; Jack Schneider, Director of Education, Maritime Aquarium.

Picture Credits (t = top, b = bottom, l = left, r = right)
Hammerhead on cover (Amos Nachoum/Corbis), coral on cover (Jeff Hunter/Getty Images), 6–7 (Grant V Faint/Getty Images), 8b (Jan Derk), 11t (Ron & Valerie Taylor/ANTPhoto.com), 11bl (Bill Bachman/ANTPhoto.com), 12 (Kelvin Aitken/ANTPhoto.com), 13 (courtesy of the Great Barrier Reef Marine Park Authority), 16b (Kelvin Aitken/ANTPhoto.com), 19t (Paddy Ryan), 20–21 (Gary Bell/Zefa/Corbis), 22 (courtesy of Mark Rosenstein), 23t (Adrian Pingstone), 25r (Uwe Kils), 27 (Matt Wright), 28 (Stephen Frink/Getty Images), 29l (Rudie Kuiter/ANTPhoto.com), 30–31 (Jeff Hunter/Getty Images), 32 (2) (Ron & Valerie Taylor/ANTPhoto.com), 32 (3) (courtesy of the Monterey Bay Aquarium), 32 (4) (Richard Ling).

The Great Barrier Reef

MY UNDERSEA ADVENTURE

This book is different from any you have read
before. It is the journal I kept while on an
amazing undersea adventure. I set off to look
for my great-grandfather's lost gold watch.
But while searching for it, I discovered the
riches of the Great Barrier Reef.

TABLE OF CONTENTS

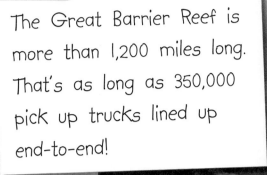

The Great Barrier Reef is more than 1,200 miles long. That's as long as 350,000 pick up trucks lined up end-to-end!

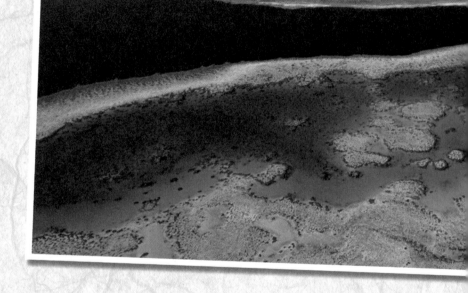

RESEARCH AT THE REEF

I just arrived at the Great Barrier Reef along the northeastern coast of Australia. My father is a marine biologist. He is here doing research on the plants and animals that live in the ocean

GREAT
BARRIER
REEF

AUSTRALIA

The Great Barrier Reef from the air

around the reef. It's here that my great-grandfather, also a marine biologist, lost his gold watch almost 100 years ago. That's what I've come to find.

IT'S ALIVE!

I am doing some reading before going scuba diving tomorrow. I just learned that the Great Barrier Reef is the world's largest coral reef system. It can even be seen from outer space! And the coral that makes up the reef is actually alive. The hard part on the outside protects a tiny animal called a coral polyp (POL-ip). Some coral polyps are smaller than the head of a pin.

Orange sun coral

Elkhorn coral

Coral comes in all shapes and sizes. There is even a type of coral called brain coral because it looks like a human brain!

Brain coral

Red cauliflower coral polyps at night

Coral eats in two ways. By day, it shares the food made by the algae that live inside it. At night, it sticks out its tiny tentacles to catch tiny plants and animals as they float by.

The Great Barrier Reef is home to several different kinds of sea turtles, including green, leatherback, and hawksbill turtles. The hawksbill turtle is known for its beautiful shell. People used to hunt it for its shell. Now so few are left, it is an endangered species.

Hawksbill turtle

TONS OF TURTLES

I'm hoping to see some of the reef's amazing turtles. My father says I should keep an eye out for a leatherback turtle. These turtles can be 7 feet long and weigh 1,200 pounds!

Giant leatherback turtle with diver

Green turtle

Leatherback turtle building a nest to lay its eggs

Like all sea turtles, the leatherback lays its
eggs on the beach. The babies hurry to the
sea after they hatch.

THE UGLIEST MERMAIDS

Today we are diving in the ocean. I'm a little nervous. There are some big and dangerous animals out there. I'm hoping to see the giant but gentle dugong (do-GONG), or sea cow.

Dugong eating sea grass

Dugongs are mammals, not fish. They give birth to live babies and need to come to the surface to breathe. Dugongs don't eat meat, only sea grass. So I'd be safe if I met one.

Dugong with baby, called a calf

Believe it or not, sailors may have thought that dugongs were mermaids. They may have seen dugongs with sea grass, which looked like long hair, on their heads.

There are about 3,000 different types of nudibranchs. Each has a favorite food, such as sponges or coral. Some even eat other nudibranchs!

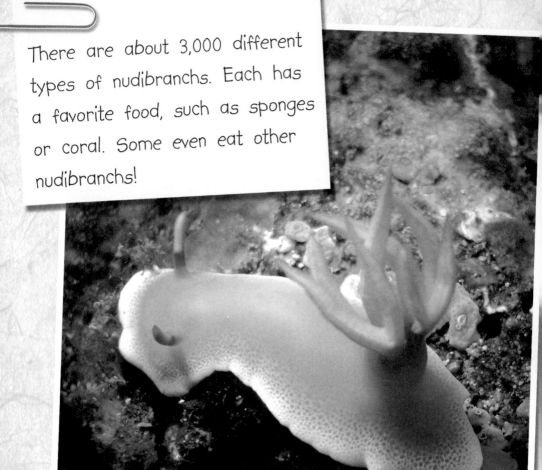

Nudibranch crawling on coral

OCEAN NIGHTLIGHTS

Looking for the lost watch, I've been keeping an eye out for anything gold. That's how I found a nudibranch, also called a sea slug. Nudibranchs are snails, but they don't have shells. They do have ways to protect themselves, however. Some animals avoid them because of their bright colors. The colors send the message that these snails may be poisonous. Some nudibranchs can also sting by using stinging cells they get from some sea animals they eat!

Nudibranch with black lines

Spanish dancer nudibranch

Nudibranch raises its head

EEL APPEAL

Diving this morning, I saw something scary stick its head out from between two rocks. My father said it was probably a moray eel. Moray eels eat crabs, fish, and squid.

Fimbriated Moray Eel

Moray eels have small eyes and can't see well. They rely on their sense of smell to help them catch food.

Giant Moray Eel

They have sharp teeth and are sometimes covered in a thin layer of poison. I felt lucky to get away!

Green Moray Eel sticking its head out of a hiding place

Sea anemones have tentacles that sting, but clown fish are not hurt by them. Other fish are, so they stay away. This is how the sea anemone protects the clown fish.

Clown fish together with a sea anemone

FRIENDS AND ANEMONES

Today I saw a colorful clown fish snuggled up in a sea anemone (eh-NEH-meh-nee). They live together and help each other.

Sea anemone

Clown fish

The anemone keeps the fish safe. And the fish cleans the anemone and brings it food. Even underwater creatures share!

EIGHT-ARMED DANGER

Last night my dad had a talk with me. He warned me not to put my hands into cracks in the coral reef—even if I saw great-grandfather's watch. He said some dangerous sea creatures hide in these cracks.

1 Blue-ringed octopus in motion. It is squirting water to push itself forward.

2

Today I saw a small octopus hiding in a crack. It looked harmless, but I was careful not to touch it. When it saw me, it turned bright yellow with blue spots! Dad said it was a blue-ringed octopus warning me to stay away.

The blue-ringed octopus turns color as a warning: "Stay away. I'm poisonous!" The bite of this octopus can kill a person in just a few minutes. Even its spit is deadly!

3

A FISH WITH A BITE

Today I saw a triggerfish "dig" for clams to eat. It did this by squirting water out of its mouth and flapping its fins. This stirred up the water around the clam and lifted the clam out of its

Titan triggerfish are good hunters. Smaller fish sometimes follow them just to eat their leftovers.

Titan triggerfish about to look for clams

bed. The triggerfish then used its strong jaws and sharp teeth to crush the clamshell. No wonder divers are warned to keep their hands away from this fish!

Picasso triggerfish

Clown triggerfish

Humpback whale breaching

GENTLE GIANTS

What a thrill! I saw a humpback whale today! It jumped out of the water and landed with a giant splash. This is called breaching.

A humpback whale can eat 5,000 pounds of food in a single day! But it only eats during half the year. During the other half, it lives off the fat stored in its body.

Krill (actual size)

Humpback whales are huge. One whale can weigh as much as 11 elephants! Yet they eat mostly very tiny creatures called krill.

Blue Linckia starfish

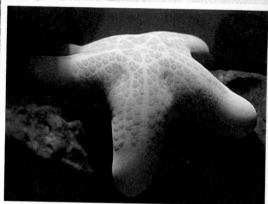
Starfish on a rock

STARS OF THE REEF

Today was an important day. My father and his team found a big group of crown-of-thorns starfish. These starfish are a problem for the reef. They eat the hard coral and can ruin the reef.

The Great Barrier Reef is home to other kinds of starfish, too. They come in different shapes and colors. The one I liked was blue and had five arms. Dad said that if a starfish loses an arm, another arm grows back in its place!

The crown-of-thorns starfish has sharp spikes. The spikes are poisonous to people and some sea creatures.

Crown-of-thorns starfish on coral

Sea horses can change color to match the things around them. This helps them hide from their enemies.

Two sea horses attached to coral

HORSES OF THE SEA

I've seen sea horses in fish tanks. Today I saw sea horses in the sea! It was hard to see them because they looked a lot like the coral. They were attached to the coral by their tails.

I still haven't found great-grandfather's watch . . .

When a sea horse has babies, it's the father who gives birth!

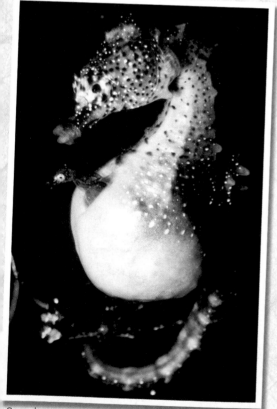

Sea horse giving birth

Sea horse

REEF TREASURES

I woke up to a surprise today. Dad had left some letters on my pillow. They were from my great-grandfather! He wrote them long ago to his mother. He wrote about losing the watch. The letters also told of all the great

sea life he saw in the reef. The last letter said he valued the creatures of the Great Barrier Reef more than gold. I didn't find his watch, but I think I discovered the real treasure.

SHARKS OF THE REEF

Many types of sharks swim in the waters around the Great Barrier Reef, including those shown below.

GREY NURSE SHARK
This shark nests in underwater caves during the day and only comes out at night.

GREAT HAMMERHEAD SHARK
This shark gets its name from the odd shape of its head.

ZEBRA SHARK
This shark has stripes like a zebra when it's young, but it has spots like a leopard when it grows up.

WHITETIP REEF SHARK
This shark is named for the white tips on its back and tail fins.